BISHOP WESTCOTT
AND THE
PLATONIC TRADITION

BY

DAVID NEWSOME

The Bishop Westcott
Memorial Lecture
1968

CAMBRIDGE
AT THE UNIVERSITY PRESS
1969

CAMBRIDGE UNIVERSITY PRESS
Cambridge, New York, Melbourne, Madrid, Cape Town, Singapore, São Paulo, Delhi

Cambridge University Press
The Edinburgh Building, Cambridge CB2 8RU, UK

Published in the United States of America by Cambridge University Press, New York

www.cambridge.org
Information on this title: www.cambridge.org/9780521076531

© Cambridge University Press 1969

First published 1969
Re-issued in this digitally printed version 2008

A catalogue record for this publication is available from the British Library

ISBN 978-0-521-07653-1 paperback

'ASSUREDLY not every one who saith "Plato, Plato"', John Morley once observed, 'is admitted to that intellectual kingdom.'[1] The remark is incontestable, I think you would agree; and it is true not only of self-styled Platonists who are pleased to see themselves as continuators of a noble tradition or who take refuge in the shelter of a great name, but also of those for whom the claim is made by historians and commentators who love to categorise and are perhaps rather too inclined to suppose that what a man has studied in his formative years he retains without substantial modification to the end of his days. The nineteenth century saw many English men of letters who could be described as Platonists. It is a little disturbing, however, to note the extraordinary range of answers supplied by twentieth-century scholars to the question: which of these writers would you select as the *quintessential* Platonist? Dean Inge has given pride of place to Wordsworth, because of his concept of the poetic imagination;[2] A. E. Taylor would appear to favour John Ruskin because the social message of *Fors Clavigera* was the purest interpretation in that century of the teaching of *The Laws*

3

and the *Republic*.[3] The American classical scholar, the late Professor Paul Shorey, unhesitatingly selected John Stuart Mill who had the clearest understanding of the meaning of 'dialectic',[4] and our own Sir Ernest Barker sang the praises of Carlyle, because he had the most vivid sense of the spiritual reality of the universe and combined this with a healthy contempt for the evils of democracy.[5] An equally strong case could be made out for Coleridge, Shelley, Jowett, F. D. Maurice, Matthew Arnold or Walter Pater.

Enough has been said, however, to establish my point. Can all these great originals really belong to the same philosophical tradition? Only, it would seem, if one admits very considerable variations in the interpretation of the tradition itself. That this is undoubtedly so, we shall hope to substantiate presently. The one sure thing that can be said is that in the nineteenth century the Greek philosophers really came into their own, and—as the century progressed—this renaissance seemed to represent a victory for the Platonists. Even Aristotelian Oxford which had nurtured that master rhetorician, John Henry Newman, and the archetypal schoolman, William Ewart Gladstone, succumbed to the Socratic spell in the second half of the century. Who could have foreseen it? Certainly not their ancestors of the Augustan Age, who had admired the Roman virtues, cultivated a Latin style and shown as scant respect for the giants of Greek antiquity as the befuddled medieval translator of a series of Greek texts who represented Alcibiades as a seductive damsel wooed by Alexander the Great and, after blinking uncomprehendingly at Aristotle's *Posterior Analytics*, supplied the ingenious, if intriguing, rendering of its title as 'The Book of the Behinds'.[6]

Of course John Morley, in deprecating the taking of Plato's name in vain, was not lashing out wildly. He had Emerson in particular in mind, of whom he thought very little—an opinion shared by Hort and Westcott, it may be observed in passing.[7] Also the agnostic in him made him understandably resent the irritating habit of many contemporary churchmen of appealing to Plato as a witness to Christian truth. As is well known, this was by no means a specifically nineteenth-century phenomenon. Indeed, if it is valid to make a distinction between Plato himself and the philosophical tradition to which his writings gave rise, then the Christian claim both to belong to that tradition and to interpret it for successive generations is a very sound one. Even to regard Plato himself as one of the prophets, which Westcott was inclined to do, is not completely absurd. It is true that one would have to omit from the canon the fact that Plato in the *Phaedo* was indiscreet enough to let Socrates ask Crito to sacrifice a cock for him to Asclepius,[8] and one might have to gloss over Plato's conception of the

Godhead in the *Republic*, which represented the Almighty as both unbending and unbendable, a Being not to be propitiated by 'mendicant prophets' or timely repentance.[9] The whole point of Socrates' reply to Glaucon and Adeimantus was that 'virtue is its own reward'. On the other hand Plato did look beyond the traditional pantheon (he had Hesiod rather than Homer in mind), pouring scorn upon 'stories of the King of Heaven eating his infant son in order to avoid the danger of dethronement, and the son later retaliating by castrating his parent',[10] and sought something that would more plainly answer to the needs of man. The real anticipation of the Christian revelation in his writings was—as Dr Paul Shorey pointed out—not what the Neo-Platonist made of his teaching on the immortality of the soul, the nature of Divine Judgement and the doctrine of recollection through the myth in the *Phaedrus* of the heavenly procession and the winged charioteer, but the simple message, which was expressed so succinctly by Matthew Arnold, that 'conduct is three-fourths of life'. An even purer rendering of the essence of Platonic ethical teaching comes in the words of Christ: 'What shall it profit a man to gain the whole world and lose his own soul?'[11]

Now the Neo-Platonists would not leave well alone. They elaborated Plato—most particularly the Plato of the *Parmenides*, the *Phaedo* and the *Timaeus*

—rather as the medieval schoolmen 'went to town' on Aristotle. A gap appeared to exist between the doctrine of the Forms and the idea of God; so first Plotinus, and finally Proclus, must attempt to bridge it by inventing 'scales of being' and 'ladders of perfection'. The poetry and symbolism of Plato became the subject of 'obsessed meditation or of hairsplitting refinements of dialectics'.[12] All was subordinated to 'the passion for a fully articulated vision of the world as a structural unity'.[13] Finally, the intuitionism of Plato came to be regarded less as a means of discerning Truth and more as a mystical process towards the contemplation of the Ineffable One. Dean Inge, in his Hulsean Lectures of 1925, chose to define Platonism in the words of Professor J. A. Stewart thus: 'Platonism is the mood of one who has a curious eye for the endless variety of this visible and temporal world, and a fine sense of its beauties, yet is haunted by the presence of an invisible and eternal world behind, or, when the mood is most pressing, within the visible and temporal world, and sustaining both it and himself—a world not perceived as external to himself, but inwardly lived by him, as that with which in moments of ecstasy, or even habitually, he is become one. This is how personal Platonism, whether in a Plotinus or in a Wordsworth, may be described in outline.'[14]

Well, this is a pretty woolly definition, but it has

some relation to Platonism, one would have to admit. The key words—'mood', 'ecstasy'—were the words which attracted the late Dean of St Paul's, student as he was of Plotinus and—at the time that he first enunciated it at least—the rather solitary advocate of the mystical way. So let us clarify our first point. In the nineteenth century, there were Platonists like Coleridge and Maurice who were intuitionists, Platonists like Mill and Ruskin who wanted to reform the world, Platonists like Matthew Arnold—and before him, Coleridge again—who were moralists and enunciated a doctrine of the élite. But there were Platonists also who, although they may have shared one, more or even all of these notions with those who were prominent in their time in expressing them, were attracted by the more mysterious and elusive elements in Plato—the myths and the symbolism, the apprehension of the world of the unseen, the notion of the One behind the Many, the transcendentalism. For them Plato was not the anti-democrat, the moralist or the social reformer. He was—as Basil Willey put it— 'the Orphic enthusiast who longs to be delivered from the wheel of life, and to enter the realm of essence where the soul's true pasturage is to be found'.[15] Coleridge, as usual, supplies us with the clue, when he complained how habitually men confounded Platonists with Plotinists.[16] The Romantic Poets were, on the whole, Plotinists; those throughout the history of the Western World who have followed the Plato of tradition rather than the Plato of the Dialogues have been Plotinists; Dean Inge's Hulsean Lectures were concerned with Plotinists; and it is to this number that Brooke Foss Westcott properly belongs.

There is, however, one other complication. If the pure, clean water of classical Platonism had been converted into a heady wine by the Romantic poets, so that much of what passed for Platonism in the nineteenth century was more properly a distillation of the metaphysical elements in the Dialogues following the tradition of the Neo-Platonists, the effects of adulteration at the hands of German philosophers, and most notably Hegel, was to add another subtle flavouring to the brew. In the second half of the century (and possibly before as well) it becomes insufficient to guard against the confounding of Platonist with Plotinist; you have to disentangle the teaching of Plato from the interpretations of the Neo-Hegelians. This task is exceedingly complex. In the first place, the traditional guides have let us down. Pfleiderer, in his general survey, tells us nothing of this; and neither René Wellek in his study of Kantian influences, nor Professor Muirhead in his attempt to chart the impact of Hegelianism on Anglo-Saxon philosophy, has appeared even to recognise that the problem exists—that is to say, how much of Victorian Platonism was in fact (to change our metaphor of the liquids) Hegelianism grafted upon a Coleridgean stock?[17] Secondly, too much emphasis has perhaps been laid on the direct impact of the Hegelian translations and commentaries on Oxford philosophy in the late decades of the nineteenth century. Of course the influence of Hegel on Jowett was profound. He was certainly studying Hegel as early as 1845, and he came in time to regard the German philosopher as the greatest interpreter of Plato in all history.[18] 'He has done more to explain Greek thought', he wrote in his introduction to the *Sophist*, 'than all other writers put together.'[19] The dominance of T. H. Green, an avowed Germanist, though not uncritical of Hegel,[20] and then of Edward Caird meant that Oxford men were set on the quest of scaling the Absolute by the ladder of Dialectic practically until the end of the century.

But, of course, there is more to it than this. German ideas were infiltrating for some time before the great Hegelian debates of the closing decades—of the *fin de siècle*, some classical scholars would say, questioning whether philosophy in general and Plato studies in particular benefited from the experience, echoing the opinion of John Stuart Mill that too much conversancy with Hegelian dialectic tended to deprave the intellect.[21] Matthew Arnold's Platonism, for instance, which occasionally has a German ring about it (how else could such an urbane writer substitute for the simple monosyllable 'God' the ludicrously unattractive formula 'The Eternal Power not-ourselves, that makes for righteousness'?),[22] was drawing liberally from Fichte and Spinoza; and, it may well be, as Dr Roth has indicated, that much of what seemed in Hegel to make sense to the English mind was what Hegel had himself derived from Spinoza.[23] Too little consideration is given also to the Cambridge Platonists of the nineteenth century, who in the persons of Coleridge and Julius Hare, and to a lesser extent F. D. Maurice, were more familiar with German writings than their Oxford contemporaries. We may illustrate the point by taking one particular Hegelian concept—his teaching on the Unity of Contradictions—which is encountered very frequently in the writings of Victorian Platonists.

Now let us begin with Westcott himself. There are two characteristics of Westcott's mind which—if he had been an Hegelian—would be easily explained. In the first place, his understanding of Truth was that it was never to be found in the mean position, but always at the extremes. It was the union of polarities. Arthur Benson noted this characteristic attitude of mind showing itself time and time again in the Sunday afternoon conversazioni at King's which it was Westcott's custom to hold during term when he was Regius Professor.

'Nothing ever seemed to please him more than to confront two apparently contradictory truths.' 'I don't know what to think', said a simple-minded undergraduate to him once, on some such occasion; 'both these statements seem true, and yet, either excludes the other.' 'Yes, that is so', said the Professor with a brilliant smile. 'I am always so thankful when I can get down to a contradiction—then I really feel I am on safe ground.'[24]

That this was very much more than donnish affectation we shall see in a moment. It is interesting, however, to note that the second characteristic is—as it were—the rider of the first. If truth is a contradiction (or—in Hegelian terms—if, as one advances into the higher logic, apparent differences merge), then one's apprehension of truth must be well served by looking for it in the most improbable places, and particularly in the place where you would least expect to find it—in the argument of your absolute opponent. It is hard to put this into words without using Mauricean terminology, because it is—as you will know—the very essence of Maurice's theology. Every prophet, party, sect or Church sees a portion of the truth and proclaims it; but what it proclaims becomes a half-truth if it denies the truth of its opponents. Find the half-truth that your opponent has seen, and add it to the portion of truth that you have perceived, and you may get the whole truth. Now look at the opening sentences of Westcott's essay on 'Positivism' which forms the first Appendix to his *Gospel of the Resurrection*: 'No religion can fail to be a fruitful subject of study. Even the rudest reveals something of the natural feelings and wants of man which are awakened by the experience of life. And exactly as we believe Christianity to be *the* Truth, we shall confidently expect to find in it all that is true in the manifold expressions of human thought. Thus it has happened not unfrequently that independent speculation or instinctive aspirations have brought out elements in the Gospel which had been before overlooked or set aside. They were there, and even actively at work, but they were not consciously apprehended.'[25] He goes on to point out the hidden truth in Positivism which Christian opponents had too often failed to perceive.

A more exact enunciation of the concept comes as early as his school days in Birmingham, when—according to his brother-in-law—he went out of his way to study Mormonism on the ground that 'all excesses and mischievous delusions among men come from one-sided views of truth, and too great importance given to one aspect of it, or else from people's assertion of party needs: that the way to combat error was to seek the element of good in it'.[26]

It is quite certain that this idea had nothing to do with Hegelianism; it is very doubtful, in view of the early expression of it, that it was derived from the teachings of F. D. Maurice where it is so plentifully to be found. One hesitates to add anything to what is becoming something of a 'chestnut' as a controversy—was Westcott right in asserting that he read only one book by Maurice and read no more for fear of jeopardising his own independence of mind? The answer is 'no'. If it would be helpful, I could add a few more instances to those which Dr Vidler cited on this occasion four years ago[27]—for instance, Westcott had certainly read Maurice's *Moral and Metaphysical Philosophy*, where the bulk of his Platonism can be found[28]—but I assure you that it would be a waste of all our time. To pick a phrase from the rubbish-heap of what sometimes passes for scholarship amongst the *avant-garde*, it is a 'non-problem'. What *is* instructive, in this connection, is the fact that Maurice believed that this teaching on the Unity of Contradictions was essentially Platonic. In a rather vapid way, it is. It is certainly the subject of discussion in the *Parmenides*, the *Theaetetus* and the *Sophist*, the dialogues which show a mounting preoccupation with metaphysics and a corresponding diminution of the poetic element. Jowett enthused greatly over the Hegelian quality of these later dialogues, and wrote in his introduction to the *Sophist*, that in this dialogue 'the kindred spirit of Hegel seems to find . . . the crown and summit of the Platonic philosophy—here was the place at which

Plato most nearly approached to the Hegelian identity of Being and Not-Being.'[29] Also one might say that if, as Plato believed, truth—when once the mists were pierced by the mind's eye of the philosopher—turned out to be something simple, harmonious, pure, as it must have been at the beginning of time before there was a distinction between things seen and things unseen, then the quest for truth must involve the appreciation that all contradictions of the visible world are in fact illusory.

Nevertheless Maurice admits that Plato never actually says so. The totality of his teaching confirms it. According to his own testimony this was the interpretation of Plato conveyed by Julius Hare. Hare taught his pupils, Maurice wrote, that 'there is a way out of party opinions which is not a compromise between them, but which is implied in both, and of which each is bearing witness'. Then again, 'Hare did not tell us this...Plato himself does not say it; he makes us feel it.'[30] The previous owner of my second-hand copy of the *Life of F. D. Maurice*, from which this quotation is taken, has scribbled knowingly in the margin: 'This is Hegel.' Well, if it is—Maurice was unaware of it. The only German opinion on Plato which Maurice respected, he once told Hort, was that of Schleiermacher.[31]

Hare's knowledge of German was, of course, considerable. At the end of his life, he had collected in his library some 3,000 German books. At the time that he was teaching F. D. Maurice (1825) he had certainly read some Hegel, though the only quotation from Hegel's writings in the portion of *Guesses at Truth* which Hare himself contributed was a reference to the *Philosophy of Law*.[32] At any rate, the most obvious source from which Hare might glean this interpretation of Plato—and the same would hold true of Maurice and Westcott, despite their rather modified rapture for the 'sage of Highgate'[33]—was Coleridge. At the end of this long, and I hope not too tedious, excursion into the obscurities of Neo-Hegelianism, we come back to the much-quoted remark of Coleridge that 'men are usually right in what they affirm and wrong in what they deny', an aphorism which Maurice admitted that he took much to heart;[34] and this rather less well-known, though equally instructive, passage from the *Table-Talk*: 'He (Plato) leads you to see, that propositions involving in themselves a contradiction in terms, are nevertheless true; and which, therefore, must belong to a higher logic—that of ideas in the Aristotelian logic, which is the instrument of the understanding.'[35] Perhaps Coleridge caught it from the Germans; possibly from Schelling. No matter. This, at least, is an answer to the undergraduate's bewilderment at Westcott's seemingly perverse delight in contradictions. It was part of a recognised Platonic tradition.

But where did Westcott get his ideas from? They were, after all, somewhat limited in their range, based on deep reading and precise study of language, rather than on a wide coverage and the richness of personal experience. Scott Holland complained of 'a sameness' in everything that Westcott wrote. 'Wherever you open his books, he is sure to be saying what he always said.'[36] Arthur Benson noted that a pernicketiness over the meaning of words gave to Westcott's writings a resemblance to 'the French definition of metaphysics as the act of bewildering oneself methodically'.[37] He knew the classics well and could recite great chunks of them by rote, but he had none of the prodigious reading-power of contemporaries like Macaulay, Mill or Matthew Arnold. When he read a new author, it was because someone suggested that he ought to do so. According to Llewellyn Davies, Westcott's reading of Comte, Ruskin, Maurice and Browning all came late—after he had heard his friends enthusing over their merits.[38] The Platonism may have come quite early. One of the subjects which he chose for a paper to the Philological Society at Trinity, when he was an undergraduate in the 1840s, was 'the Eleatic School of Philosophy',[39] which must have entailed a reading of the *Parmenides*, although in an early letter to E. W. Benson, in August 1850, he taxed him 'for certain unnatural calumnies against the Stagirite', in terms which suggested a higher opinion of Aristotle than of Plato.[40]

During his eighteen years as an assistant-master at Harrow, the direction of his future studies seems to have become firmly set. It was during this time that he wrote for the *Contemporary Review* the articles on the myths of Plato, Aeschylus and Euripides which were later included in his *Essays on the History of Religious Thought in the West*, and his theology became rooted in the Gospel of St John. The passion for Robert Browning dates from the 1860s, when Westcott in a Harrow classroom opened the eyes of a future headmaster of Charterhouse to the hidden depths and inner revelations of 'The Grammarian's Funeral'.[41] Although physically at Harrow, his heart was in Cambridge, where Hort and Lightfoot were delivering the lecture-courses which he dearly longed to give, and in two fields that Cambridge hoped to make their own at that time, his help was being earnestly solicited. The first, and most famous, was the project for the Commentary on the New Testament, and the second—less well known —was the venture proposed by Hort, for a translation of the whole of the Dialogues of Plato. The second scheme came to naught, possibly because of Westcott's unwillingness to participate but mainly because word reached Cambridge that Jowett of Balliol had already got under way.[42]

So a new Plato, and perhaps too a new Platonism,

came forth from Oxford, as should never have been. And the true heirs of Coleridge and Maurice returned to their biblical studies. Then the sense of joy which had sprung up in the heart of Erasmus, and the rapture which had carried away the young Shelley into flights of poetic fancy (or—if you prefer it—that airy nonsense which intoxicants can induce people to accept as truth), were re-lived by countless young men strolling by the banks of the Isis in search of glades and groves in which to indulge the new taste for a sophisticated dialectic. The times were propitious. Plato is irresistible if you read Aristotle first (as most Oxford men had done). Matthew Arnold had created a romanticised Platonism which actually *identified* the source of 'sweetness and light' as the *genius loci* of Oxford; and if the urbane 'Oxford manner' which this new vogue of Platonism did so much to create[43] sometimes sounded (in the prose of its chief advocate) suspiciously like the phrases and cadences of John Henry Newman in the pulpit of St Mary's,[44] then the fact that their model had been trained as an Aristotelian was not held against him. The inflection was right, even if the logic was that of a schoolman or a Goth. Scott Holland had come up from Eton, imbued with Platonism for life from the gentle influence of William Cory. Gore had come from Harrow and was probably a Platonist before he fell under the sway of T. H. Green, although the evidence that he derived much from Westcott at school, apart from the attraction of asceticism, is very slight.[45] Undoubtedly both found the Oxford of the early 1870s intensely congenial. There Platonism flowered in the mood of joyous optimism, which all the reminiscences of the period love to recall.

'We never stopped laughing', Holland said, as he looked back.[46] The reign of Mill was over, and his Logic went out of fashion almost overnight.[47] T. H. Green taught on idealism which, although sometimes obscure, was both a call to action and an exhortation to love one's fellow-men. It is not to be forgotten either (for the influence is sometimes overlooked) that in 1870 John Ruskin returned to Oxford as Slade Professor of Art, and for thirteen years was to complement the teaching of T. H. Green in his lectures on the ideals of art and beauty and the need for 'comprehensive social and economic reconstruction'.[48] The mood of the era is expressed thus in the luxuriant prose of Scott Holland as he writes of the so-called 'Holy Party', the circle of friends—Gore, Paget, Lyttelton, Illingworth and Moberly—who were later to present their composite thoughts on the doctrine of the Incarnation in *Lux Mundi*. The prose, you will note, is as much of its period as the sentiment—young dons on reading parties, blissfully aware that time is on their side and the world is very beautiful.

'There were no invading cares. There were no duties...We were complete in ourselves: we owed nothing to anybody: we were a band of friends who were sufficient for each other: and we wanted nothing more. Round us the loveliness of some selected fairy spot ringed us in. The hills waited upon us: the rivers ran for us: the great sea laughed as we plunged into its green Cornish waters. Nature was on our side: and we were one with it. These were the magic hours, that fed our lips with honeydew. To me they will be always the symbol and the expression of all that can make this earth the joyous home of health, and beauty, and friendship.' Francis Paget, when at rare moments serious discussion had set in, would bring the company back to sanity and laughter: 'We would think whether anybody could be found to meet Dr King's demand and write a new "Summa Theologica". Who would do it? Perhaps Swallow, the learned Cuddesdon Chaplain? "No", said Paget, "not quite. It is not every Swallow that can make a Summa."'[49]

The great sea laughed as they plunged into its waters. Nature was on their side. They were one with it—these phrases are the clue to the Incarnationalism of the closing years of the nineteenth century. That florid passage of Scott Holland is quite as fundamental to an understanding of late-Victorian theology as any single text that could be cited from the pages of *Lux Mundi*. In fact I should go further: this essay on Francis Paget, together with N. S. Talbot's opening essay to *Foundations*, where the same note of buoyant hope is sounded in the midst of the storm-clouds of impending war, chart the history of modern Incarnationalism for us with incomparable power: the battle is won even before it begins; through 'the Word made Flesh' comes assurance that Nature is on our side and we are on its; man is elevated to a new dignity by the divine act; the potentiality of man has the blessing of God upon it. And why? Because of the union of God and man in the Logos. The Gospeller of this Logos is St John; the prophet and philosopher of the Logos is seen to be Plato; the poet of the Logos who in their own time had found the words and the imagery to express their ultimate aspirations is Robert Browning.

Westcott would take the occasional plunge into the great sea—from a Normandy beach rather than Cornwall, as a matter of fact—but it is not on record that the waters laughed, even metaphorically. Rather did the onlookers, as they saw the grotesquely unepiscopal figure in a striped red bathing costume hurling himself with a sort of frenzied purposefulness into an activity which the mass of men regard as recreational.[50] But he belonged to an older generation and could never have been carefree. His Hellenism was toughened by a deeply Hebraic strain. Apart from this, however, the affinity in thought with the *Lux Mundi* group is remarkable. There was virtually no cross-fertilisation, as far as I can see. Although Scott Holland and Gore were to join forces with Westcott in 1889 with the foundation of the Christian Social Union, this was not the outcome of some earlier theological or philosophical synthesis between Oxford and Cambridge Platonists, nor was it the self-conscious merger of social teaching derived respectively from F. D. Maurice and T. H. Green. While the incarnational theologies of Westcott and the Holy Party were so similar in laying the emphasis on the exaltation of the powers and potentialities of man (as opposed to the earlier incarnationalism of the Tractarians who had tended to stress the divine nature of Christ almost to Docetic lengths), their work was carried out entirely independently. Westcott did not develop his incarnationalism into a Kenotic theory as Gore did, even though both scholars held in high esteem the authority of Origen, from whose writings Gore drew so liberally in his presentation of the meaning and history of Kenosis.[51] I have not seen it observed before that Westcott deliberately refrained from reading *Lux Mundi* on its publication,[52] and had apparently not rectified the omission as late as 1894.[53] In fact I find no evidence at all, apart from one very doubtful allusion in *Lessons from Work*, that he ever *did* read it. And this is surely more extraordinary than his alleged reluctance to acquaint himself with the writings of F. D. Maurice.

Behind the two theologies lies a common respect for the same witnesses to Christian truth. The point is best illustrated by a remark of William Temple, which appeared in the Preface to *Mens Creatrix*: 'It is said of Bishop Westcott [he writes] that he held in especial veneration St John, Origen and Browning. I do not in any way claim comparison with that great scholar and seer if I say that the first name and the third, with Plato's in place of Origen's, would designate the master-influences upon my own thought.'[54] The substitution by Temple of Plato's name for Origen's should not be taken very seriously. Westcott came to Origen via Plato and saw him as the greatest exponent of Platonic idealism before the light went out of the world with the triumphant emergence of Aristotelian realism at the time of the Emperor Justinian.[55] There were two supreme elements in Origen's teaching, both of which were derived from Plato and the Fourth Gospel—the first was the realisation 'that the whole world is a manifestation of the goodness and righteousness of God in every detail', and the second, the teaching 'that the moral determination of each individual is a decisive element in the working out of the divine counsel'. He continued: 'This compound conception of the sum of finite being as a unity consistent with, or rather dependent upon, the free and responsible action of each individual, is evidently of the utmost significance. There can be none greater.'[56]

Would that the world had cherished such teaching for all time! But it was not to be. The pernicious element which caused the teaching of Origen to be submerged was the influence of St Augustine—the shadow of whose power Westcott represented as 'perilous to the growth of truth'.[57] The tragedy occurred mainly because of St Augustine's ignorance of Greek. He was a Latin thinker, more than that, an African. 'He looked at everything from the side of law and not of freedom; from the side of GOD, as an irresponsible Sovereign, and not of man, as a loving servant. In spite of his admiration for Plato he was driven by a passion for system to fix, to externalise, to freeze every idea into a rigid shape. In spite of his genius he could not shake off the influence of a legal and rhetorical training, which controversy called into active service...The arguments by which he trusted to win men for the Church was a coarse representation of future rewards and punishments. The centre of his whole dogmatic theory is sin.'[58]

Westcott's favourite passage from Plato is the supreme contradiction of this attitude. It is the conversation between Socrates and Simmias in the *Phaedo*, when Socrates reflects on his feelings of deep happiness before he goes to his death. It is indeed one of the finest passages in all literature; and for the benefit of those who think of Plato in the guise with which mid-twentieth-century controversy has ventured to present him—as the Fascist precursor of Adolf Hitler—I give you an extract from it now. Socrates is speaking: 'Will you not allow that I have as much of the spirit of prophecy in me as the swans? For they, when they perceive that they must die, having sung all their life long, do then sing more than ever, rejoicing in the thought that they are about to go to the God whose ministers they are. But men, because they are themselves afraid of death, slanderously affirm of the swans that they sing a lament at the last, not considering that no bird sings when cold, or hungry, or in pain...Because they are sacred to Apollo, and have the gift of prophecy, and anticipate the good things of another world, therefore they sing and rejoice in that day more than ever they did before. And I too, believing myself to be the consecrated servant of the same God...would not go out of life less merrily than the swans.'

Then Simmias replies in this vein. In our present life, we cannot really know about these promises of the next world. Certitude would seem impossible. 'Yet I should deem him a coward who did not prove what is said about them [i.e. the promises] to the uttermost, or whose heart failed him before he had examined them on every side. For he should persevere until he has attained one of two things: either he should discover or learn the truth about them; or, if this is impossible, I would have him take the best and most irrefragable of human notions, and let this be the raft upon which he sails through life—not without risk, as I admit, if he cannot find some word of God which will more surely and safely carry him.'[59]

What is this Word of God which man might find, floating on the raft of his noblest aspirations, or in Matthew Arnold's phrase 'walking by the best light we have'? In the divine *Logos*, Westcott answers, we have that 'securer stay'.[60] In the fourth Gospel, the hope of Socrates becomes the firm faith of the Christian. And this is why Christianity is, indeed, the 'Absolute Religion'. It speaks most perfectly to the needs of man. For 'the Word became flesh and dwelt among us'. Christ came 'to effect the perfection no less than the redemption of finite being,... to bring a perfect unity of humanity without destroying the personality of any one man'.[61] And again: 'The Incarnation and the Resurrection furnish the basis for a religion which is intensely human, and which, at any moment, introduces the infinite and the unseen into a vital connexion with the things of earth—a religion which illuminates the dark clouds that lie over our work, which offers an ideal wherein we can recognise the fulfilment of the destiny of humanity, which supplies an inspiration of power flowing from a divine fellowship—a religion, in other words, which is a complete satisfaction of the religious needs of man.'[62]

Westcott perceived the *poetic* quality in Plato. The myths which he so frequently employs are not 'simply graceful embellishments of an argument. They are truly philosophic, because they answer to the innate wants of man; they are truly poetic, because they are in thought creative.'[63] Likewise, to Westcott, the Gospel of St John was essentially 'a poem, because it is the simple utterance of a mind which received into itself most deeply and reproduced most simply absolute truth'.[64] In his own day the poetic representation of these same eternal truths was the peculiar genius of Robert Browning. Westcott was devoted to Browning. Indeed Sir W. B. Richmond, who conversed at length with Westcott during the sittings for the portrait which now hangs in the Fitzwilliam Museum, came to the conclusion that the two men, the theologian and the poet, had very much the same cast of mind. It was not only that they shared 'the same love of the transcendental', the same passion 'for all that belongs to our race—its faults, its struggles, enterprises, and failures', but that they also strove to express these feelings, if not through the same medium, at least through the same process of thought. Both men perceived the truth as through the intuitive instinct of a child, but neither was capable of communicating the simple vision to others, without having recourse at times to 'symbolic obscurity', and—as it were—putting language to the torture.[65] It was one of the greatest thrills of Westcott's life that, when he was presented to the Honorary D.D. degree at Edinburgh in 1884, he found that Browning was standing next behind him at the presentation. They conversed for a short while, and Westcott extracted a promise from the poet to send him certain lines, written in his own hand, from two of his poems— 'The Pope' and 'Guido'.[66]

Westcott's writings are studded with Browning quotations, almost as liberally as those of William Temple. Three passages occur most frequently. The first, and most often quoted—so often, indeed, that he occasionally misquotes it—are the following lines, from *Death in the Desert* where Browning points to the understanding of love (as he does so frequently) as the ultimate concern of our existence:

'Life, with all it yields of joy and woe,
And hope and fear, ...
Is just our chance o' the prize of learning love
How love might be, hath been indeed, and is.'[67]

From *Fra Lippo Lippi*, comes a passage where Browning points to that spring of essential goodness, welling up within the soul of the world, even though, to the outward eye, all is sordid, cruel and corrupt:

29

'This world's no blot for us
Nor blank: it means intensely, and means good;
To find the meaning is my meat and drink.'[68]

Indeed that is the function of the poet, the theologian—the artist. The artist's vision reveals that same principle of human love, silently working beneath the surface:

'We're made so that we love.
First when we see them painted, things we've
    passed
Perhaps a hundred times nor cared to see;...
...Art was given for that.
God uses us to help each other so,
Lending our minds out.'[69]

We may strive and fail; only at the last shall we see the inadequacy of the endeavours of this life as compared to the fullness of the life to come. As it is expressed in *Abt Vogler*: 'on the earth the broken arcs; in the heaven a perfect round.'[70]

There is a great deal more to Browning than this, of course—a very strong sense of individualism, a candour in his treatment of the passionate nature of love and a revolt against so many of the conventions of his time—that Westcott forbore to comment upon, even if he ever discerned these other elements. To him, Browning was the true poet who saw 'the infinite in things'; who perceived hope in wretchedness and ugliness; who pointed to the central truth that life is a whole, a unity.[71] The kinship is most marked, however, in their common Platonism—the vision of the eternal or the infinite within the material and the temporal. Truth to Browning was the intuitive flash of recognition. Ideal love, as portrayed in the *Flight of the Duchess*, the *Last Ride Together*, the *Statue and the Bust*, was itself intuitive perception between two people, leading them at once away from the things of the world into spiritual union. As Mr E. D. H. Johnson has shown, the famous refrain of *Pippa Passes*,

> 'God's in his heaven—
> All's right with the world',

is not to be taken as the quintessential expression of mid-Victorian optimism. It is nothing of the kind. It is rather the affirmation of the simple wisdom of the child, of the young innocent, who through her faith in ultimate goodness enables the worldly and the corrupt to see themselves as they are and to feel guilty and ashamed at the superior perception of the child. 'In Browning's world, the prophets and artists, the lovers and doers of great deeds are never primarily remarkable for intellectual prowess. Their supremacy is the result of a genius for experiencing life intuitively. They possess a phenomenal capacity for passionate emotion, combined with a childlike reliance on instinct...Whether it be Fra Lippo, or Rabbi Ben Ezra, or David in *Saul*, or the

Grammarian, or Childe Roland, Browning's heroes are always the children of their intuition.'[72]

Now if our picture of Westcott's Platonism is to aspire to something more than a broken arc itself and reach towards the perfect round, we must say one brief word about his politics. Plato was most assuredly an anti-democrat; and in twentieth-century controversy, he appears to us too often in the guise of the advocate of totalitarianism, and particularly of the extreme right-wing brand. Westcott, on the other hand, styled himself a socialist. There may seem something of a paradox here. To use a technical term, Westcott's understanding of the nature of society was holistic. Like Plato, he believed that the whole was superior to, and greater than, the parts. In his famous definition of Socialism, which he gave at the meeting of the Church Congress at Hull in October 1890, he rejected the notion that Socialism had to do with the battle of the classes or the economic rearrangement of the nation's wealth. It was, more properly, 'a theory of life'. 'In this sense Socialism is the opposite of Individualism, and it is by contrast with Individualism that the true character of Socialism can best be discerned. Individualism and Socialism correspond with opposite views of humanity as made up of disconnected or warring atoms; Socialism regards it as an organic whole, a vital unity formed by the combination of contributary members mutually interdependent.'[73]

Now this is very Platonic; and it is also precisely what Professor Karl Popper has attacked as Plato's 'Collectivism', pointing out that Plato consistently confused 'individualism' with 'egoism' and 'Collectivism' with 'altruism'. 'For Plato and for most Platonists, an altruistic individualism...cannot exist. According to Plato, the only alternative to collectivism is egoism; he simply identifies all altruism with collectivism, and all individualism with egoism.'[74] It may be a just criticism, although Plato, who can rarely be accused of using words loosely, doubtless meant precisely what he said. And Westcott too, or, for that matter, all thinkers who have conceived of society as a mighty organism directing or directed towards a moral end—from a conservative like Edmund Burke, who certainly regarded the state as a creation greater than the sum of its parts, to a Fabian like H. G. Wells, whose reading of Plato first brought home to him 'the conception of a society in which economic individualism was overruled entirely in the common interest'.[75]

No high moral appeal could have left Westcott unmoved. Rigorous teachers had seized his youth (Prince Lee and Arnold), and if they had not purged his faith, they had plainly indicated that truth, although often simple, is never easily attained. Westcott, with his deep yearning for asceticism, would never have wished it otherwise. Perhaps part of the appeal of the so-called *Socratici viri* to the Victorians was precisely the underlying notion that a philosopher really has to be a saint. He must love others and undergo pain and deprivation both in the quest for truth and more importantly in his duty to communicate it to his generation. With West-cott this self-denying principle is met at every turn; it becomes at times, like Keble's humility, almost over-bearing; too demanding; perhaps even a little deficient, as Arthur Benson so delicately suggests,[76] in the gift of spontaneous love for one's fellowmen that will show itself in accepting their weaknesses and limitations, while making the most of the refractory material of which mankind is made. If so, it was the weakness of the age. As G. M. Young so delightfully put it, the Victorians often forgot that at the head of the Ten Commandments should have been written the rubric: 'Candidates should attempt the fifth and the seventh, and at least three others.'[77]

Westcott was satisfied with nothing less than ten. Just as Socrates upbraided Adeimantus in the *Republic* for equating happiness with the revelries at a peasants' feast,[78] so Westcott preached that a full life was a life of perseverance. In 1849 he wrote to the young girl who was to be his wife: 'To live is not to be gay or idle or restless. Frivolity, inactivity, and aimlessness seem equally remote from the true idea of living. I should say that we live only so far as we cultivate all our faculties, and improve all our advantages for God's glory.'[79]

Posterity would pass the judgement. What had they made of their 'brief time of toil'?[80] One must always look to the end. As Browning put it, in *The Last Ride Together* (and thereby summing up the full genius and vigour of the whole Victorian age):

'All labour, yet no less
Bear up beneath their unsuccess.
Look at the end of work, contrast
The petty Done, the Undone vast.'

NOTES

1 J. Morley, *Critical Miscellanies* (1886), I, 308.
2 W. R. Inge, *The Platonic Tradition in English Religious Thought* (1926), pp. 74, 78–9.
3 A. E. Taylor, *Platonism and its Influence* (1925), p. 91.
4 Paul Shorey, *Platonism, Ancient and Modern* (Berkeley, California, 1938), pp. 231–2.
5 Joseph E. Baker (editor), *The Reinterpretation of Victorian Literature* (Princeton, 1950), p. 224.
6 Paul Shorey, *op. cit.* p. 90.
7 A. F. Hort, *Life and Letters of Fenton John Anthony Hort* (1896), I, 164; A. Westcott, *Life and Letters of Brooke Foss Westcott* (1903), II, 49–50.
8 *Phaedo*, p. 118 (all references to Platonic dialogues are made to the four-volume 1871 edition of Benjamin Jowett).
9 *Republic*, p. 364.
10 R. W. Livingstone, *Greek Ideals and Modern Life* (Oxford, 1935), p. 51.

11 Paul Shorey, *op. cit.* p. 72.

12 *Ibid.* p. 46.

13 A. E. Taylor, *op. cit.* p. 12.

14 W. R. Inge, *op. cit.* p. 69.

15 Basil Willey, *The English Moralists* (1964), p. 50.

16 Paul Shorey, *op. cit.* p. 232.

17 O. Pfleiderer, *The Development of Theology in Germany since Kant and its Progress in Great Britain since 1825* (1890), esp. pp. 303–401; René Wellek, *Kant in England, 1793–1836* (Princeton, 1931); J. H. Muirhead, *The Platonic Tradition in Anglo-Saxon Philosophy: Studies in the History of Idealism in England and America* (2nd edition 1965), esp. pp. 147–73.

18 E. Abbott and L. Campbell, *The Life and Letters of Benjamin Jowett* (1897), I, 117.

19 *Ibid.* II, 250.

20 E.g. of Hegel's acceptance of the holistic concept in Plato's thought, see the interesting discussion of this in Melvin Richter, *The Politics of Conscience: T. H. Green and his Age* (1964), p. 203.

21 Paul Shorey, *op. cit.* p. 38.

22 Matthew Arnold, *Literature and Dogma. An Essay towards a Better Apprehension of the Bible* (5th edition 1876), p. 401. See the delightful comments on Matthew Arnold's lack of judgement in this respect in A. C. Benson, *The Leaves of the Tree: Studies in Biography* (1911), p. 410.

23 In 'Spinoza in recent English Thought' in *Mind*, xxxvi (1927), quoted by J. E. Baker, 'Our New Hellenic Renaissance' in *The Reinterpretation of Victorian Literature*, edited Joseph E. Baker (Princeton, 1950), p. 221.

24 A. C. Benson, *op. cit.* p. 48.

25 B. F. Westcott, 'Aspects of Positivism in relation to Christianity' in *The Gospel of the Resurrection: Thoughts on its Relation to Reason and History* (8th edition 1902), p. 211.

26 Arthur Westcott, *op. cit.* I, 19.

27 A. R. Vidler, *F. D. Maurice and Company* (1966), p. 275.

28 B. F. Westcott, *Essays in the History of Religious Thought in*

the West (1891), note 48, contains a lengthy quotation on Plato from Maurice's *Moral and Metaphysical Philosophy*.

29 B. Jowett, *Dialogues of Plato* (1871), III, 445.
30 F. Maurice, *Life of Frederick Denison Maurice* (1884), I, 56.
31 *Ibid.* II, 38.
32 *Guesses at Truth, by Two Brothers* (1866 edition), p. 118. This part, acknowledged to be one of Julius' portions through the signing by the letter 'U' (see introductory memoir by E. H. Plumptre, XXIV), was written in 1825.
33 A. Westcott, *op. cit.* I, 111. Compare also F. Maurice, *op. cit.* I, 251. 'Coleridge was not a thorough Platonist...'
34 F. Maurice, *op. cit.* I, 343.
35 S. T. Coleridge, *Table-Talk* (30 April 1830), quoted in P. Shorey, *op. cit.* p. 224.
36 Henry Scott Holland, *Personal Studies* (1905), p. 131.
37 A. C. Benson, *op. cit.* p. 33.
38 Joseph Clayton, *Bishop Westcott* (1906), pp. 184–5.
39 A. Westcott, *op. cit.* I, 47.
40 *Ibid.* I, 165.
41 *Ibid.* I, 197.
42 A. Hort, *op. cit.* I, 424. See also I, 349.
43 A claim made by the late Master of Merton College, Mr G. R. G. Mure, in 'Oxford and Philosophy' in *Philosophy*, XII (1937), 300–1.
44 For a very full comparison between Matthew Arnold and Newman, see David J. Delaura, 'Matthew Arnold and John Henry Newman. The Oxford Sentiment and the Religion of the Future' in *Studies in Literature and Language* (University of Texas), VI, Supplement 1965, 573–702.
45 Discussed in my Gore Memorial Lecture 'The Assault on Mammon, Charles Gore and John Neville Figgis' in *Journal of Ecclesiastical History*, XVII, no. 2 (October 1966), 238–40.
46 Henry Scott Holland, *A Bundle of Memories* (1915), p. 62.
47 James Carpenter, *Gore. A Study in Liberal Catholic Thought* (1960), p. 28.

48 William S. Knickerbocker, 'Victorian Education and the Idea of Culture' in J. E. Baker, *op. cit.* p. 126.

49 Henry Scott Holland, *op. cit.* pp. 64–5.

50 A. C. Benson, *op. cit.* pp. 28–9, describes the incident alluded to here.

51 See especially Charles Gore, *Dissertations on Subjects connected with the Incarnation* (1895), pp. 114–20.

52 A. Westcott, *op. cit.* II, 68.

53 *Ibid.* II, 226.

54 William Temple, *Mens Creatrix. An Essay* (1917), p. vii.

55 B. F. Westcott, *Essays in the History of Religious Thought in the West*, p. 222.

56 *Ibid.* p. 238.

57 *Ibid.* p. 250.

58 *Ibid.* pp. 246–7.

59 *Phaedo*, pp. 84–5.

60 B. F. Westcott, *Essays in the History of Religious Thought*, p. 50. See also p. 139 where the quotation is repeated in the essay on Euripides. Compare *The Gospel of the Resurrection: Thoughts on its Relation to Reason and History* (1902 edition), p. 130.

61 B. F. Westcott, *Essays in the History of Religious Thought*, p. 345.

62 *Ibid.* pp. 348–9.

63 *Ibid.* p. 2.

64 B. F. Westcott, *An Introduction to the Study of the Gospels* (8th edition 1955), p. 277.

65 A. Westcott, *op. cit.* II, 34.

66 *Ibid.* II, 4. The lines were *The Pope*, ll. 2116 ff.; *Guido* (2), ll. 2425 f.

67 E.g. B. F. Westcott, 'On some points in Browning's view of life' in *Essays in the History of Religious Thought*, p. 255; in his address to the Y.M.C.A. at Auckland Castle in 1891, 'A Quiet Life: its joy and power', in B. F. Westcott, *The Incarnation and Common Life* (1893), p. 330; misquoted in his sermon at St Andrew's, Deptford, in 1891, 'A Gospel

for the Poor' in *ibid.* p. 302. He says, 'Life with all it *brings of joy or woe...*'

68 E.g. B. F. Westcott, 'The Relation of Christianity to Art' in *Essays in the History of Religious Thought*, p. 330; compare also speech at Sedbergh in 1896 in *Christian Aspects of Life* (1901), p. 381.

69 *Essays in the History of Religious Thought*, p. 331. Compare the phraseology in the lecture on 'Ideals' in *The Incarnation and Common Life*, p. 144, preceding a quotation from *Abt Vogler*, where Westcott surely has the passage from *Fra Lippo* in mind. See the comparable context of this quotation in Richard Brook's essay on 'The Bible' in *Foundations*, edited B. H. Streeter (1913), p. 64; also William Temple, *Mens Creatrix*, pp. 123, 131.

70 B. F. Westcott, *The Incarnation and Common Life*, p. 144. See the discussion of this poem by one of its greatest admirers in William Temple, *Mens Creatrix*, pp. 97–8.

71 B. F. Westcott, *Essays*, pp. 253–4, 256.

72 E. D. H. Johnson, *The Alien Vision of Victorian Poetry. Sources of the Poetic Imagination in Tennyson, Browning and Arnold* (Princeton, 1952), pp. 86–7, 92–3.

73 B. F. Westcott, *The Incarnation and Common Life*, p. 226.

74 K. R. Popper, *The Open Society and its Enemies* (3rd edition 1957), I, 101.

75 R. W. Livingstone, *op. cit.* p. 34.

76 A. C. Benson, *op. cit.* pp. 56–7.

77 G. M. Young, *Daylight and Champaign* (1948 edition), p. 248.

78 *Republic*, p. 420.

79 A. Westcott, *op. cit.* I, 145.

80 *Ibid.* I, 355.

This lecture was given in Cambridge on 7 November 1968

For EU product safety concerns, contact us at Calle de José Abascal, 56–1°,
28003 Madrid, Spain or eugpsr@cambridge.org.

www.ingramcontent.com/pod-product-compliance
Ingram Content Group UK Ltd.
Pitfield, Milton Keynes, MK11 3LW, UK
UKHW020451240426
470322UK00016B/285